What is a Perfect World?

For Hamish and Guthrie - from Nana
For Graham, Catherine and Christopher – from Tharien

Published in Great Britain by www.NancyLynner.com

Title: *What is a Perfect World?* **by Nancy Lynner**
Illustrated by Tharien van Eck
Book design by Joyce Halsan
Production by Amanda Drollinger

Summary: What is a Perfect World? allows readers to talk about eleven different world issues with young children, and shows what important work for the world awaits.

Identifiers: ISBN 9781916901407

Subjects: Children's book-Juvenile Non-fiction- Ages 0-8; clean water; clean air; hunger; safety; medical care; world issues; UNESCO; environment; human rights; rights of the child; health; education; medical care; helping others

www.nancylynner.com
www.thariensart.com

First Edition

What is a Perfect World?

By Nancy Lynner
Illustrations by Tharien van Eck
Produced by Amanda Drollinger
Book Design by Joyce Halsan

In a perfect world...

a child h

clean air
to breathe

In a perfect world ...

a child

has

clean water

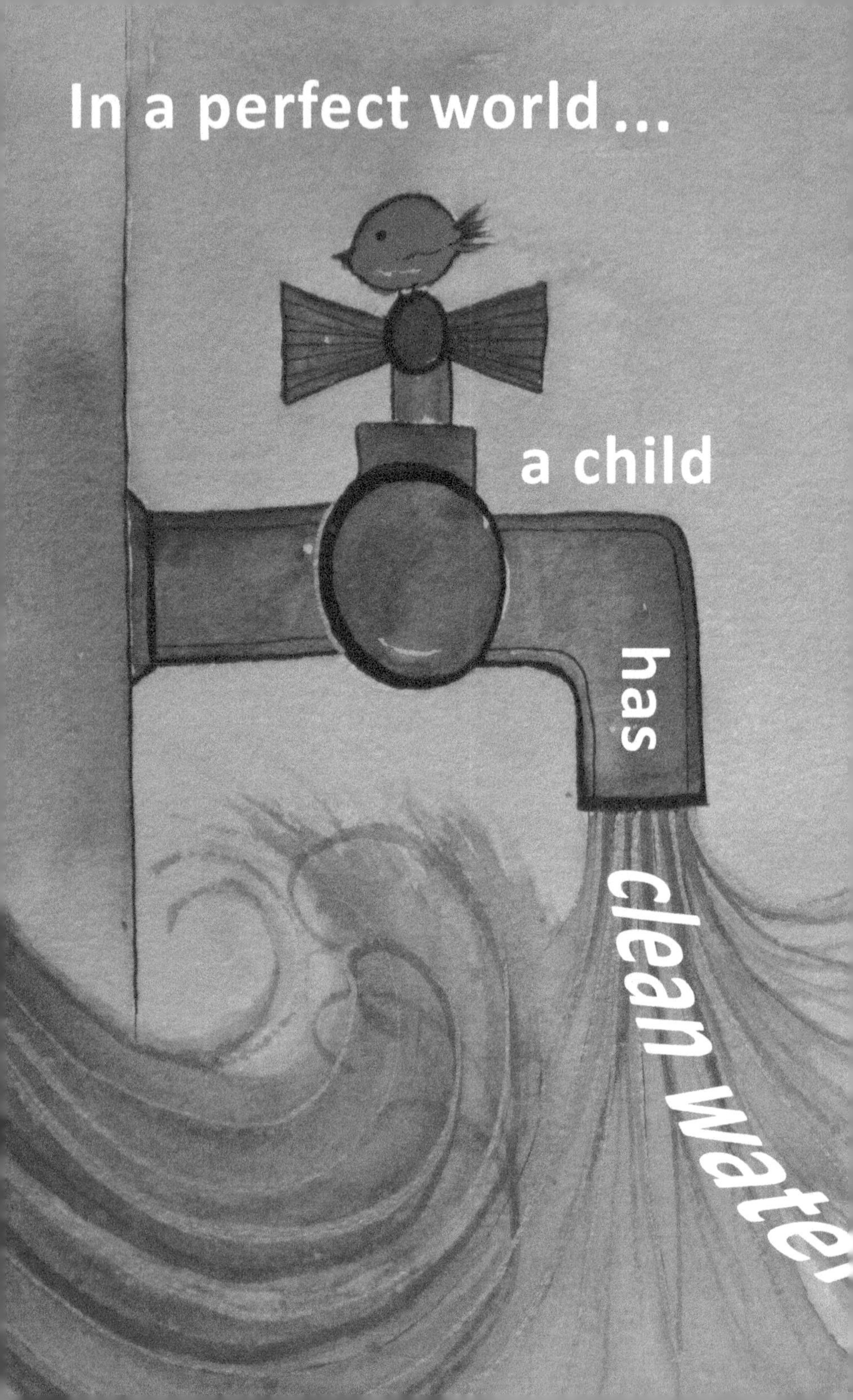

to
drink

In a perfect world...

a child
has food
to eat

when
hungry

In a perfect world...

a person
has cosy
places to
sleep
safely

In a perfect world...

a person has medical help when ill

vaccine
vacuna
yimiao
chanjo

and a mother has help...

delivering
a
baby

In a perfect world...

a child has

teachers

and

to read

In a perfect world...

a child can
run, play and

swim with
nature.

In a perfect world...
all

kin

colors

are treated fairly

In a perfect world...

a person learns

the happiness of
helping others

In a perfect world...

a person loves and

is loved

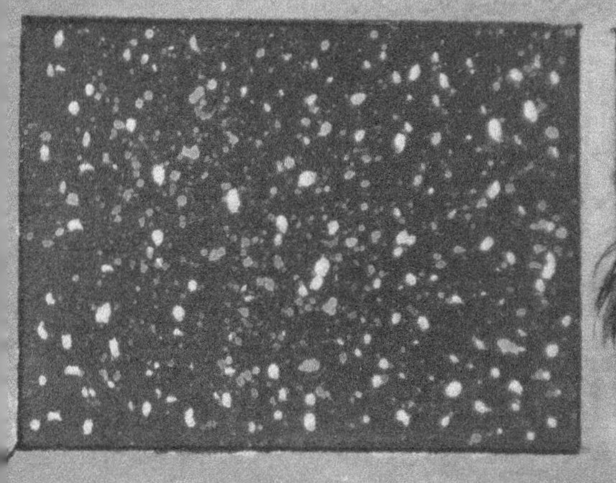

Let us make our world perfect...

together

and
as we

work
on
all
that

let
us
have

ice
cream

once
in a
while

Meet Our Friends

Upendo

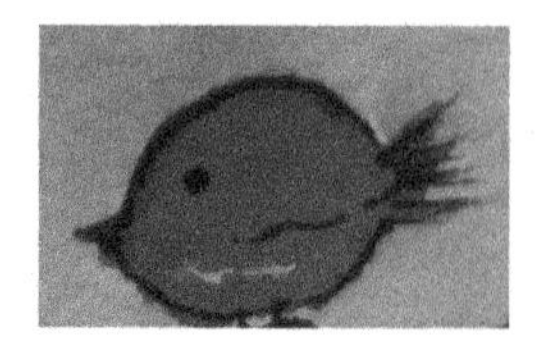

Red Bird

Mrs. Bunny
Hop Hop

Thandi

Which one are you...

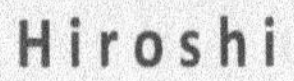

Hiroshi

Rhobi

Emma Leah

Nurse Meiling & Annabella

Dr. Amil

Baby Noah

Dr. Lyra

Xuân and Bobby

Catriona

Kavi

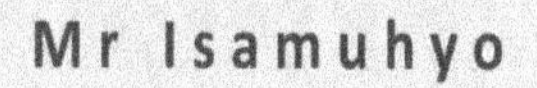

Mr Isamuhyo

Laura and Liam

Ian Peter

Cosmo

Azadeh & Arif & Zachary

Nelson James, Hannah & Sophia

Ashwini

Granny Joyce
&
amuel Andrew

Clarry
Riva

Ward Jackson &
Scott Owen

The proceeds from What is a Perfect World? will be donated to FAWCO and the FAWCO Foundation Target project in perpetuity.

FAWCO is an international network of independent volunteer clubs and associations across many countries worldwide and is a global women's NGO (non-governmental organization). The Target Program is a joint venture between FAWCO and the FAWCO Foundation, with FAWCO focusing on education and awareness while the FAWCO Foundation administers fundraising for the Target Project.

The **Target Program** (including the Target Project) follows a three-year cycle of raising awareness, project selection, monitoring and fundraising. It demonstrates the power of collaboration and increasing knowledge and awareness of global issues affecting women. The Target Programs have the overarching goal of improving the lives of women and girls on a revolving basis through four areas of interest: Education, Environment, Health and Human Rights.

This book is a collaboration between members of two of the FAWCO associated clubs: American Women's Club of Central Scotland and the American Women's Club Antwerp.

Biographies

Author: **Nancy Lynner,** M.Ed., Vanderbilt University, has a background in theatre, education, literacy and the arts. What Is a Perfect World? is Nancy's first publication for children, parents, and teachers. She worked at the Smithsonian Institution and at the John F. Kennedy Center for Performing Arts. She has taught literacy, arts, theatre and puppetry to all age groups. She lives in Edinburgh and is a member of the American Women's Club of Central Scotland.

Illustrator: **Tharien van Eck** (MBChB, DoH) is living in Antwerp in Belgium. She is a physician by training and worked as a General Practitioner and Occupational Health physician in South Africa until 2004. She then joined Johnson & Johnson, overseeing the development of workplace health programs across Europe, Middle East, Africa and Asia Pacific. She retired in 2017 and is a passionate watercolour artist and reader. She is a member of FAWCO since 2017 and is/was the Chair of the 2019-2022 Target Program focussing on Health, "Promoting Well-Being and Healthy Lives for Women and Girls".

***Producer*: Amanda Drollinge**r, has a Bachelor's of Architecture from Pratt Institute, a Masters of Architecture from University of Edinburgh and the Edinburgh College of Art. Studying Architecture in Paris at L'école Spéciale d'Architecture and in Rome. She is Director of Henderson Drollinger Architects.

Book Designer: **Joyce Halsan**, B.S. Psychology, M.Ed. in Higher Education from University of Washington. Her career includes Manager of Administrative Services in Department of Urology and Pediatrics at the University of Washington and Professor of Women's Studies and Multicultural Studies, Shoreline College, Shoreline, WA. In retirement she is Communications Convenor of the American Women's Club of Central Scotland.

Lightning Source UK Ltd.
Milton Keynes UK
UKHW020040240622
404867UK00001B/21

9 781916 901407